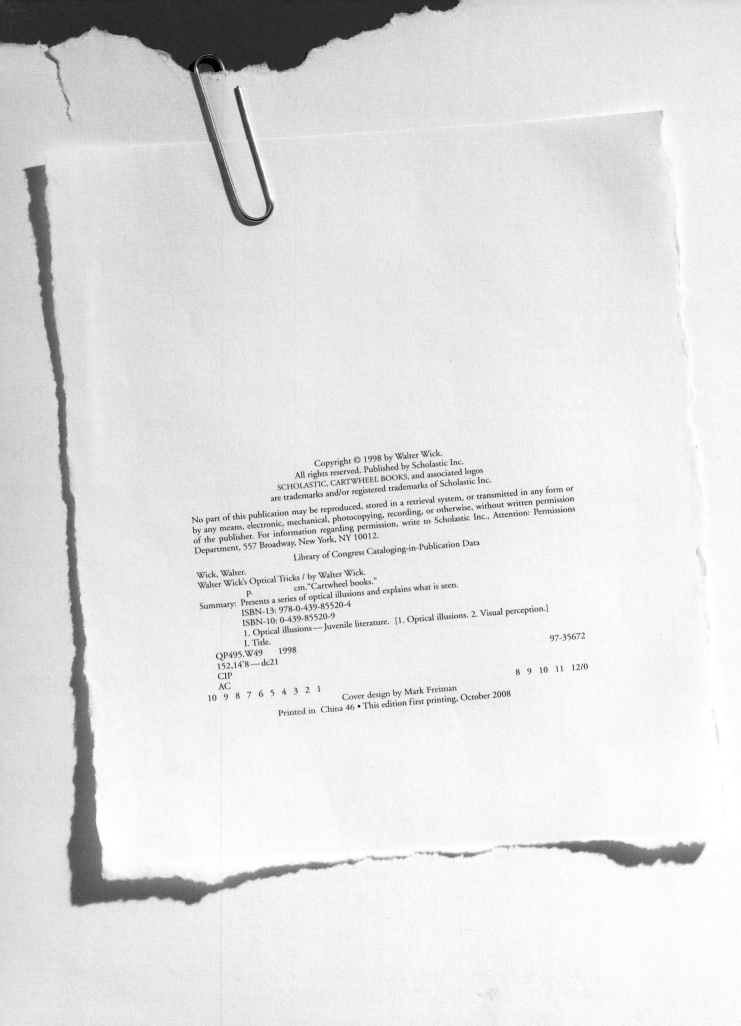

Library of Congress Cataloging-in-Publication Data

Wick, Walter.
Walter Wick's Optical Tricks / by Walter Wick.
         p.   cm."Cartwheel books."
Summary: Presents a series of optical illusions and explains what is seen.
         ISBN-13: 978-0-439-85520-4
         ISBN-10: 0-439-85520-9
         1. Optical illusions — Juvenile literature. [1. Optical illusions. 2. Visual perception.]
         I. Title.   97-35672
     QP495.W49   1998
     152,14'8 — dc21
     CIP
     AC
10 9 8 7 6 5 4 3 2 1
                                  Cover design by Mark Freiman
             Printed in China 46 • This edition first printing, October 2008

                                                                    8   9   10   11   12/0

WALTER WICK'S
OPTICAL TRICKS

Cartwheel
·B·O·O·K·S·®

SCHOLASTIC INC.

New York Toronto London Auckland Sydney
Mexico City New Delhi Hong Kong Buenos Aires

Contents

For Linda

*Special thanks to
Dan Helt*

*and to
Grace Maccarone,
Bernette Ford,
and Edie Weinberg*

Dear Reader,

Enter the puzzling world of optical illusions, where your eyes see things that your brain misunderstands. Do you see four pieces of white paper on a yellow background? If so, you've been tricked into seeing an illusion.

Turn the book upside down to see four holes in a piece of yellow paper! Turn the book right side up, and the illusion returns.

In this book, you'll ponder impossible objects, peer into magical mirrors, and pursue phantom images. You'll find puzzles to challenge your powers of observation and clues as to how illusions work. You'll learn how your eyes play tricks with your mind and that you can't always believe what you see. You may never see things the same way again!

Walter Wick

First Impressions

A dime, a die, a skull, a screw, a 4, and more

have been pressed into clay.

Right?

Right!

Now turn the page upside down.

The clay impressions pop out!

That's an illusion.

Turn the page right side up,

and the illusion goes away.

Now try this trick.

Make a 4-inch hole in a piece of paper.

Place it on the picture

and watch the impressions pop out again.

Mirror Magic

In mirrors,

you can see around corners,

objects are only illusions,

and everything is backward!

In this mirror, one 4 is backward.

Another 4 is frontward.

Why?

While you think about that puzzle,

here's another:

How many objects were used to make

this picture?

Count with care!

The mirror's magic will deceive,

even as it provides important clues.

Go Fish!

There is something fishy about this picture.

That's because you see no fish, only fish *reflections*.

The illusion was made with three mirrors.

Can you figure out how many fish were used?

If you're floundering for an answer,

here's an important clue:

Of the fish used, no two are alike.

In Suspense

A mirror lies flat

on a tabletop,

but the objects in the mirror

seem to occupy

a strange place all their own.

An object and its reflection make a pair.

What do two halves make?

The answer is a clue

to how this illusion works.

Going Up?

Take a tour of the paradoxical pavilion.

Walk up the three little steps,

follow the walkway around to the end,

step out on the balcony,

and enjoy the view.

But wait!

You climbed only three steps

and you didn't walk uphill.

How did you get to the second story?

Tricky Triangle

The yellow triangle has a peculiar twist.

It's impossible!

Or is it?

This triangle may be tricky,

but it's not impossible.

In fact, it's not really a triangle.

Cover the top corner with your hand.

The left side goes *away* from you.

The right side comes *toward* you.

The sides are *not* joined at the top.

That's an illusion.

Turn the page and look in the mirror

for another point of view.

The Impostor

Something is not quite right in the mirror.

Study the shapes and shadows.

Look for a telltale clue.

Then pick the impostor—

one object that's not what it appears to be.

Go ahead. Choose one.

Then turn the page to see the answer.

The Deception

The big yellow box just doesn't stand up.

If it did, it would cast a dark shadow

on the orange ball.

It would also get in the way

of its own reflection.

If you thought the yellow box was bogus,

you were right.

It's not a box;

it's just three flat boards.

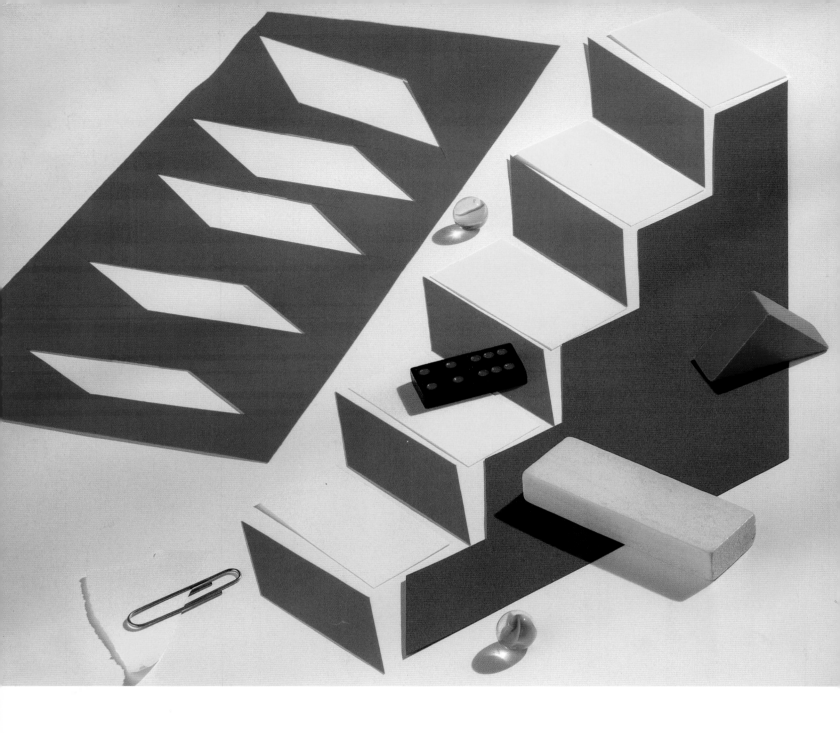

Flatland

Guess what? These stairs go nowhere.

They're just flat pieces of paper

lying flat on a surface.

On the left page, the paper pieces are loose.

On the right page, they fit together.

The shape of the stairs looks right. So what's wrong?

One clue is that objects on the blue paper look weird.

Can you find two other clues that expose the illusion?

Camouflage

The largest object in this picture

is also the hardest to see.

Look for the box behind the cat.

Cover the right side of the box with paper.

It seems to disappear.

Now take the paper away.

The checkerboard floor looks flat—

but what makes the box look like a box?

Crazy Columns

A soldier guards a mysterious ruin.

When he looks up, what will he see?

Yikes!

Can what he guards be real?

Yes.

Look at it this way.

Cover the top half of the picture.

You see round columns,

some rubble, and a soldier *reflected in* glass.

Cover the bottom half of the picture.

You see square columns *through* glass.

Now turn the page.

The Phantom of the Forest

It's a common animal

that lives in the woods

carved in wood that was never carved

with smooth, rounded edges

that are really flat.

It's an illusion!

Turn the picture upside down to find it—

The Phantom of the Forest.

More Fun With Illusions

pages 8–9

Dear Reader

Because light usually comes from above, you are in the habit of seeing shadows beneath objects. This habit is so strong, your brain is tricked into believing the shadows are beneath four separate pieces of paper. See if you can break the habit. With the picture right side up, imagine the light coming from below.

pages 10–11

First Impressions

In this picture, light comes from above, so raised objects cast shadows at their bottom edges, and impressions cast shadows on their top edges. When the picture is upside down, the position of the shadows is reversed, and your brain is tricked into seeing the impressions as raised objects.

Because the illusion can be seen when the picture is right side up, the position of the shadows can't be the only explanation. Your memory of such things as a dime, a screw, and a checker also contributes to this illusion. Your eyes see familiar shapes and shadows in the clay, and your brain recognizes them as objects, not as impressions.

pages 12–13

Mirror Magic

Mirrors reflect numbers backward, which is why the 4 on the billiard ball is backward in the reflection. Because the reverse side of the other 4 faces the mirror, it is frontward in the reflection.

Not counting the mirror itself, sixteen objects were used to make this picture. Four of the objects are obscured from view: a second checker, a large yellow marble, a large blue marble (its shadow is to the right of the 4), and a small blue marble (you may see a bit of it behind the orange ball).

pages 14–15

Go Fish!

Three mirrors are arranged in a triangle. A layer of sand covers the ground, and six fish—each with a different pattern—reflect endlessly within the mirrored walls of the triangle.

The underwater effect is an illusion created with lights. A blue-green light provided the color of ocean water, and a pale yellow light imitates sunlight shining through ocean waves.

pages 16–17

In Suspense

Two halves make a whole. Objects were cut in half and placed on the mirror. Their reflections make them appear whole again. You can see a thin line where each object meets its own reflection.

An object is rarely seen on a surface without something else seen by its side—a shadow!—but you never see shadows on mirror surfaces. You see only reflections. The absence of shadows on the mirror helps make the objects appear as if they are floating in space.

The reflective coating on this mirror, unlike most mirrors, is on the front surface of the glass instead of the back. That's why these objects appear to touch their reflections.

pages 18–19

Going Up?

The entire walkway lies flat on the ground. The "second story" is really a separate pavilion that covers the end of the walkway in the background. The balcony is attached to the arches in the foreground, but the top of the foreground archway is cut at an angle that matches the angle of the walkway's bottom edge. The shadow of the foreground archway also reveals that you can't get to the balcony from the walkway!

Tricky Triangle

pages 20–23

The mirror on page 23 shows the two disconnected pieces of the yellow "triangle." The end of one piece is flat and square; the other end is cut at an angle. A precise camera position makes those two pieces appear joined. Compare "Tricky Triangle" with the paradoxical pavilion in "Going Up?" to see how they both appear to make impossible triangles.

Curious Cube

pages 24–25

The answer is B. A cut in the front piece is just wide enough to allow the rear piece to show through. Such a precise cut is so strange and unfamiliar that the brain rejects it as improbable. Instead, the brain takes the more familiar path. It decides that the rear piece must be in front!

The Impostor/**The Deception**

pages 26–29

The sides of the three flat boards form a set of angles called a *perspective*. From a certain point of view, the boards appear to have the perspective of a box. The mirror provides a way to see the boards from that special point of view.

Flatland

pages 30–31

The paper lies flat on the surface, but the pieces are shaped to imitate the perspective of real stairs. Also, the colors were chosen to suggest the light and shadow on real stairs: yellow for bright light, red for medium, blue for shadows.

Here are two clues that expose the illusion: If the stairs were as tall as they appear, they would cast long, dark shadows. Also, like the man with binoculars, the stairs would be reflected in the steel ball.

This illusion is very similar to "The Impostor," but instead of the mirror, the camera provides the point of view that makes the stairs look real.

Camouflage

pages 32–33

The checkerboard floor was made with squares of red and white paper. The shapes on the box are not squares. The paper on the box was specially shaped to match the perspective of the floor.

Shadows help you see the box. The stronger the shadows, the more the box stands out. Without shadows, the box would disappear. Another clue: The fake squares on the box don't line up perfectly with the real squares in the background.

Crazy Columns

pages 34–37

A pane of glass, with a slightly reflective coating, stands *between* three round columns on the left and two square columns on the right. Lights were carefully placed to control what you see. Because the top of the square columns are in bright light, you can see them *through* the glass. Because the bottom of the round columns are in bright light, they are *reflected* in the glass. The brightest parts of the two sets of columns magically blend into one impossible structure.

The Phantom of the Forest

pages 38–39

At first, the fifteen wooden pieces seem like random shapes. In fact, the shapes were carefully cut to conform to a design of a deer among tree branches. Because the deer is upside down in the photograph, the wooden pieces seem separate. When the deer is right side up, it is easy to see. The shadows of the wooden pieces make the design seem to be raised, as if smooth, rounded edges have been carved in the dark wood. But this carving exists only in your mind!

About This Book

The photographs in this book were taken with 4″ x 5″ and 8″ x 10″ view cameras using Ektachrome 64T film. The models were constructed and photographed by Walter Wick with the help of his assistant, Dan Helt. Although the models and props were arranged to be deceptive, the photographs are a true representation of the objects in front of the camera. The photographs required no subsequent alterations.

As much as possible, the photographs are designed to challenge readers to compare *true perceptions* (the objects as they really exist) with *false perceptions* (the illusions) as a way to cultivate visual logic skills and to sharpen powers of observation. Some readers may have difficulty visualizing certain illusions. Others may have more trouble with how certain tricks work. The variety of ways individuals experience optical illusions is in itself an interesting area of inquiry, but it's important to keep in mind that *why* such differences occur is not fully understood—even by experts—and that each reader should experience the book at his or her own pace. The illusions in this book are not meant to be an intelligence test, but a playful and entertaining introduction to the mysteries of visual perception.

About the Author

Walter Wick is the photographer of the I Spy series of books, with more than twenty-nine million copies in print. He is author and photographer of *A Drop of Water: A Book of Science and Wonder*, which won the Boston Globe/Horn Book Award for Nonfiction, was named a Notable Children's Book by the American Library Association, and was selected as an Orbis Pictus Honor Book and a CBC/NSTA Outstanding Science Trade Book for Children. *Walter Wick's Optical Tricks*, a book of photographic illusions, was named a Best Illustrated Children's Book by the *New York Times Book Review*, was recognized as a Notable Children's Book by the American Library Association, and received many awards, including a Platinum Award from the Oppenheim Toy Portfolio, a Young Readers Award from *Scientific American*, a *Bulletin* Blue Ribbon, and a Parents' Choice Silver Honor. *Can You See What I See?*, published in 2003, appeared on the *New York Times* Bestseller List for twenty-two weeks. His most recent books in the Can You See What I See? series are *Dream Machine*, *Cool Collections*, *The Night Before Christmas*, *Once Upon a Time*, and *On a Scary Scary Night*. Mr. Wick has invented photographic games for *GAMES* magazine and photographed covers for books and magazines, including *Newsweek*, *Discover*, and *Psychology Today*. A graduate of Paier College of Art, Mr. Wick lives in Connecticut with his wife, Linda.

More information about Walter Wick is available at www.walterwick.com.